ORFOLK COUNTY COUNCIL LIBRARY AND
INFORMATION SERVICE

L LIBRARY SERVICE - BOOK PURCHASE SCHEME

WIND AND WEATHER

Barbara Taylor

Photographs by Peter Millard

FRANKLIN WATTS
London • New York • Sydney • Toronto

Design: Janet Watson

Science consultant: Dr Bryson Gore

Primary science adviser: Lillian Wright

Series editor: Debbie Fox

Editor: Roslin Mair

The author and publisher would like to thank the following children for their participation in the photography of this book: Shaniah Bart, Robin Budhathoki, Kashif Kazru, Preya Patel, Donovan Rose, Timothy Springer, Ruth Staton and Shelley Swann. Thanks to Carol Olivier of Kenmont Primary School, and Micki Swann.

Illustrations: Linda Costello

© 1991 Franklin Watts

Franklin Watts
96 Leonard Street
London EC2A 4RH

Franklin Watts Inc.
387 Park Avenue South
New York
NY 10016

Franklin Watts Australia
14 Mars Road
Lane Cove
NSW 2066

UK ISBN: 0 7496 0446 8

A CIP catalogue record for this book is available from the British Library.

Printed in Belgium

CONTENTS

This book is all about the effect of the wind on people and the environment, changes in the weather and how we measure and forecast the weather. It is divided into six sections. Each has a different coloured triangle at the corner of the page. Use these triangles to help you find the different sections.

These red triangles at the corner of the tinted panels show you where a step-by-step investigation starts.

Air on the move   4
Windy weather in everyday life

Using the wind   6
Sailing boats and windmills

Environment   8
Sand dunes; wind erosion in deserts

Plants   10
Wind pollination; seed dispersal

Air pressure   12
Pressing forces and area; effects of air pressure

Highs and lows   14
Barometers; weather maps; wet and dry weather

Measuring weather   18
Wind speed and direction; Beaufort scale; wind socks; anemometers

Forecasting weather   22
Weather stations; satellites; computer predictions

World climate   24
Weather all year round; seasons; monsoons; hurricanes

Pollution   26
Measuring air pollution; smog; greenhouse effect

More things to do   28
Did you know?   30
Glossary   31
Index   32

AIR ON THE MOVE

What happens to things around you on a windy day?

We live at the bottom of a big layer of air called the atmosphere, which surrounds the Earth. The air moves from place to place when it warms up or cools down. We call moving air the wind. Winds carry water and warmth around our world and produce the weather.

Have you ever tried to wear a hat in a strong wind? It's hard to keep the hat on your head. We often notice the wind only when it blows strongly, but it affects our lives every day. The wind influences the clothes we wear, the food we eat, where we live and how we travel. It also affects some people's jobs, such as farming or building work.

The washing dries faster on a windy day because the wind blows away the water vapour which has evaporated from the surface of the clothes.

USING THE WIND

Winds can be very powerful and people have found many ways of using wind power. The sails on these racing yachts catch the wind, which pushes the yachts along. Big sailing ships once carried people and cargoes all over the world.

Try making your own sails.

1 Find some different materials, such as cloth, paper and plastic.

2 Cut out different shapes and sizes of sails and fix them to boats made from balsa wood.

3 Blow down a straw or a cardboard tube to create a wind that pushes your boats along. Which sail makes the boat move fastest? Do the boats go faster with big sails or small ones?

Could you blow hard enough to make six windmills like this all turn at once? Large windmills have been used for centuries to grind wheat into flour, lift water and drive spinning and weaving machines. As the wind turns the sails, gear wheels turn inside the windmill. The wheels move the machinery that does the work.

Nowadays, windmills like the ones in the picture below are used to turn wind power into electricity. Unlike power stations that run on coal, gas or oil, they do not pollute the air and they use a source of energy that will not run out. But these windmills can only work in places where there are strong winds blowing most of the time. Very strong winds can also damage the windmills. Some people think they make the environment look unpleasant. What do you think?

ENVIRONMENT

Have you ever seen the wind blowing the sand on a beach? The wind changes the shape of the land by moving sand and soil around and wearing away rocks. Wind erosion is very important in deserts. In these very hot, dry places there are few plants to hold the sand and soil in place. It hardly ever rains, so water is not the most important force in shaping the land.

Sometimes the wind pushes the sand into hills called dunes, which usually move slowly in the direction the wind is blowing. If the wind blows in the same direction all year round, crescent-shaped dunes called barchans may form.

Strong winds can pick up grains of sand and drive them with a lot of force against rocks. The rough sand grains cut into the rocks just above the ground. At ground level, the moving air catches against the surface and is held back by a force called friction. It has less cutting power. Rocks may be cut into strange mushroom or pedestal shapes with a "waist" where the cutting power of the wind-blown sand is greatest.

PLANTS

Many plants, such as these plantains, rely on the wind to carry their pollen from flower to flower so that seeds can develop. In wind-pollinated flowers, the yellow sacs of pollen hang outside the flower so the wind can easily shake the pollen from them. The flowers are not usually colourful and do not have a scent but they do produce lots of pollen.

Plants such as tree mallow use insects to carry their pollen. Their flowers are brightly coloured and scented to attract the insects.

Which of these flowers do you think are wind-pollinated and which are insect-pollinated? The answer is on page 31.

Plants also use the wind to spread their seeds far and wide. If seeds move away from their parent plant they stand a better chance of finding enough light, warmth and space to grow into new plants. Some of these seeds, such as maple seeds, have wings to help them glide or spin through the air. Other seeds, such as those of poppies, are very small and light so they will easily float on the wind. When the wind blows, the seeds are shaken out of the holes around the top of the seed pod, like pepper out of a pepper pot.

AIR PRESSURE

The air all around us moves because of changes in air pressure. But what is pressure?

Try pressing the flat palm of one hand and a finger of the other hand into some modelling clay. You will find that your finger goes in much further than your hand. Pressure depends on both the amount of pressing force and the area it presses on. If the force is spread out over a large area (as it is with your hand), the pressure is reduced.

The air in the atmosphere is held close to the Earth by the force of gravity, which pulls everything on Earth down to the ground. The pull of gravity gives the air weight and the weight of all the air in the atmosphere presses down on us and everything else on Earth. We don't usually notice this air pressure because we have air inside our bodies, which presses outwards to balance the air pressure outside. The air also presses against us equally from all directions.

To prove that air pressure does exist, fill a beaker with water, place a card over the top and, holding the card carefully in place, turn the beaker upside down. You may be surprised to find that the air presses up on the card with enough force to stop the water falling out of the beaker.

Air presses up

HIGHS AND LOWS

When you blow up a beach ball, you force a lot of air inside it. This air is squashed together or compressed, so it is at a high pressure. If you take the stopper off the ball, the air inside rushes out to where the pressure is lower.

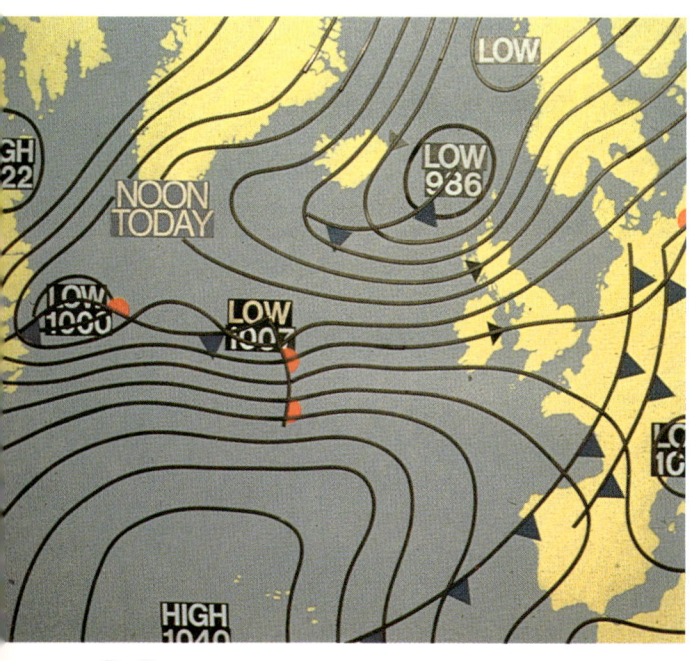

The air pressure of the atmosphere varies over time and from place to place. Winds are caused by air moving from areas of high pressure to areas of low pressure. This evens out the pressure. High pressure usually brings good weather while low pressure brings bad weather. You can find out why on pages 16 and 17. The lines on a weather map join up areas of equal pressure. They are called isobars. The closer the isobars, the more windy it will be.

14

To measure changes in air pressure, make a simple barometer.

1 Cut a piece from a balloon and stretch it over the neck of a jar or a tin. Hold the balloon in place with an elastic band.

2 Cut one end of a straw to make a pointer.

3 Fix the other end of the straw to the middle of the balloon using sticky tape. Keep the straw horizontal.

4 Mark a scale on a piece of card and stand it beside your barometer.

5 Leave the barometer somewhere out of the sun. It can be indoors or outdoors.

6 As the difference between the air pressure inside and outside the jar or tin changes, the pointer will move up and down the scale. The greater the difference, the more the pointer moves. Keep records of the weather when the air pressure is high and when it is low. How does air pressure change the weather?

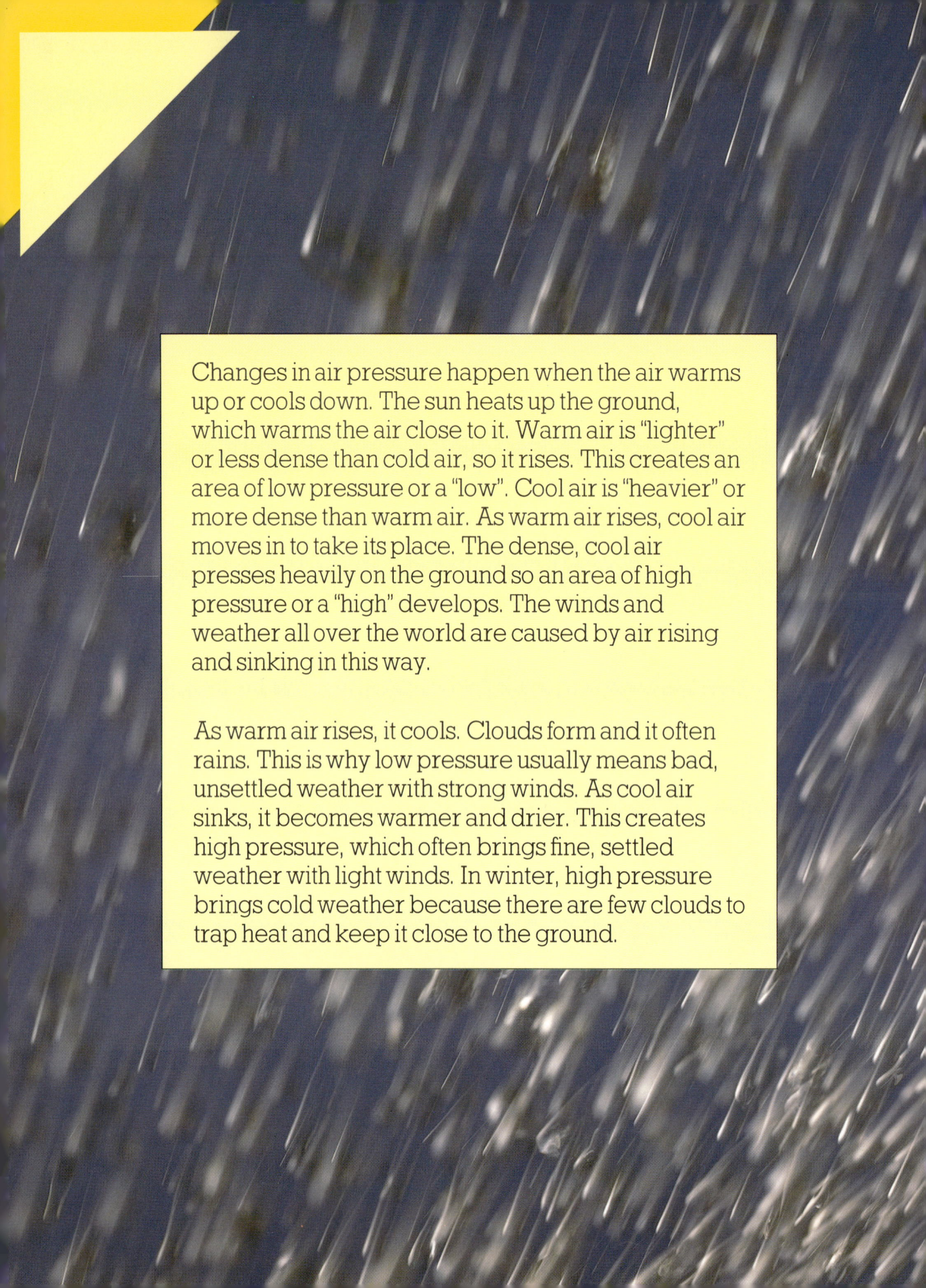

Changes in air pressure happen when the air warms up or cools down. The sun heats up the ground, which warms the air close to it. Warm air is "lighter" or less dense than cold air, so it rises. This creates an area of low pressure or a "low". Cool air is "heavier" or more dense than warm air. As warm air rises, cool air moves in to take its place. The dense, cool air presses heavily on the ground so an area of high pressure or a "high" develops. The winds and weather all over the world are caused by air rising and sinking in this way.

As warm air rises, it cools. Clouds form and it often rains. This is why low pressure usually means bad, unsettled weather with strong winds. As cool air sinks, it becomes warmer and drier. This creates high pressure, which often brings fine, settled weather with light winds. In winter, high pressure brings cold weather because there are few clouds to trap heat and keep it close to the ground.

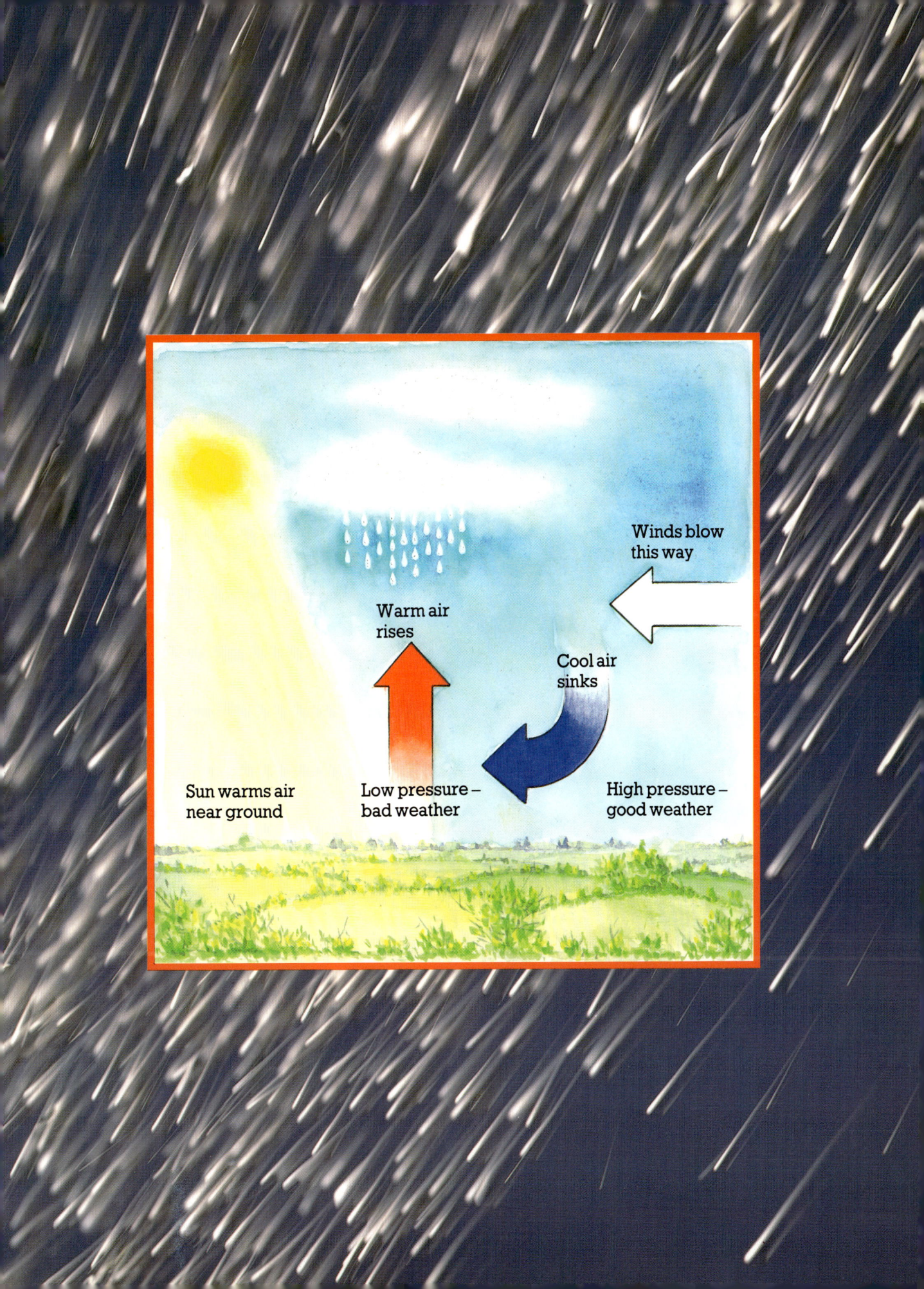

MEASURING WEATHER

1 Light air
Smoke drifts

2 Light breeze
Wind felt on face

5 Fresh breeze
Leafy bushes and small trees sway

6 Strong breeze
Hard to use umbrellas

One way of measuring the speed of the wind is to look at its effects on the local environment. Admiral Beaufort invented a scale of this type which describes the type of wind and gives numbers to evaluate the force of the wind at different speeds.

3 Gentle breeze
Light flags flap

4 Moderate breeze
"White horses" common on sea

7 Near gale
Difficult to walk in wind

8-12 Gale, storm and hurricane
Damage to buildings and countryside

19

Wind socks like this one are used to measure the wind at airports, seaports and on other open areas such as mountain roads. When the wind blows into the open end, it makes the sock point the way the wind is blowing. If the sock flaps about loosely, the wind is only light. If it sticks out in a straight line, the wind is much stronger. Information about wind speed and direction is very useful to people travelling by aeroplane or ship, and is sometimes useful to car drivers too.

See if you can design some instruments that show the speed and direction of the wind. Use different materials such as paper, cloth or plastic and try out different shapes and sizes. Put the instruments outside and use them to record the wind. How do the different materials behave when the wind blows? Which is the best design?

Make an anemometer to measure how fast the wind blows.

1 Glue two long thin pieces of balsa wood into a cross shape and fix a piece of dowel or a round pencil under the centre of the cross.

2 Fix a cotton reel inside a lidded cardboard box using sticky tape or modelling clay.

3 Make a hole in the lid of the box and push the dowel or pencil through the hole and into the cotton reel. Make sure it can spin round.

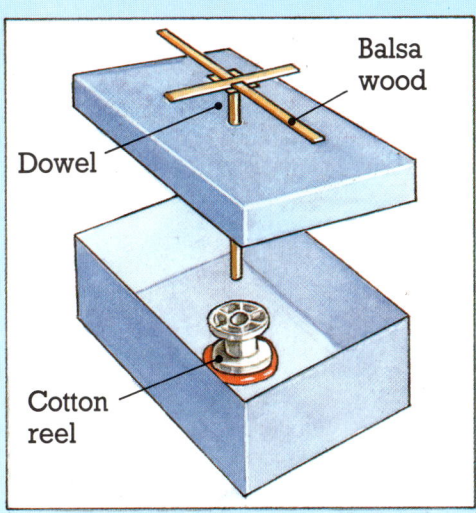

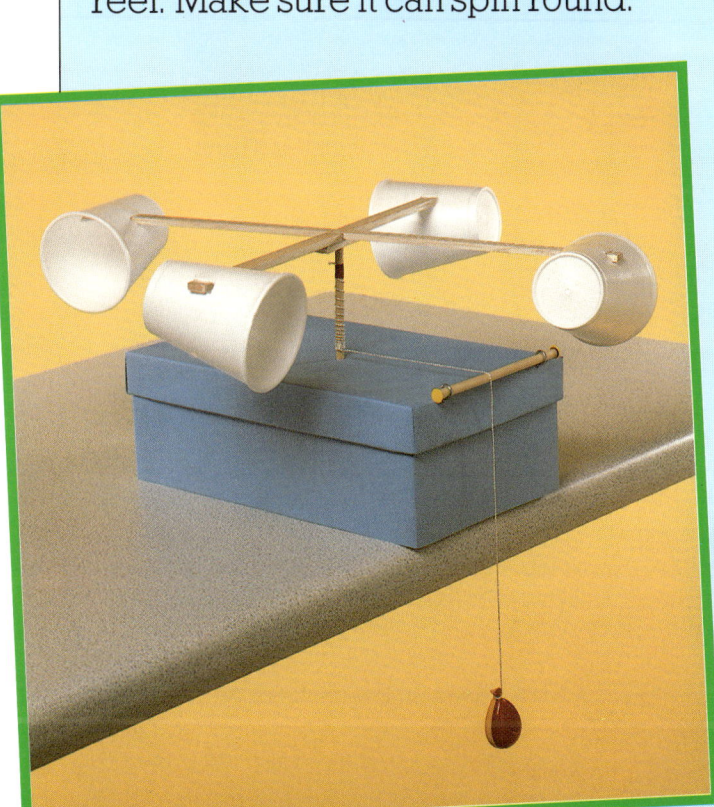

4 At one end of the box, fix another piece of dowel or a round pencil so it lies parallel to the edge of the box, using pins or curtain eyes. It needs to be able to turn round.

5 Attach a long piece of string to the dowel under the cross and wind it round and round the dowel. Tie a small weight on the other end of the string and hang it over the dowel or pencil at the end of the box.

6 Push four plastic cups on the ends of the balsa wood cross.

7 Put your anemometer outside on a table or another surface off the ground. When the wind blows, time how long the weight takes to move up and down. This will give you some idea of the wind speed. Record your results over several weeks and draw up a wind speed chart.

21

FORECASTING WEATHER

By measuring and studying the weather, people are able to forecast how it will change in the future. Scientists who study the weather are called meteorologists. They make careful measurements of all the different aspects of the weather – temperature, rainfall, air pressure, wind speed and direction, cloud cover, humidity (moisture in the air), and sunshine.

This information is collected from weather stations, weather balloons high up in the atmosphere, satellites out in space and ships at sea. The satellite photograph on the next page shows a severe storm covering most of the British Isles.

By feeding all this information into computers and plotting the results on maps, meteorologists can forecast the weather all over the world. Although these forecasts are usually fairly accurate, they are not perfect. The weather may change after the forecast has been made, or a piece of vital information may be missing. You could make your own weather station and see how accurate the local weather forecasts really are.

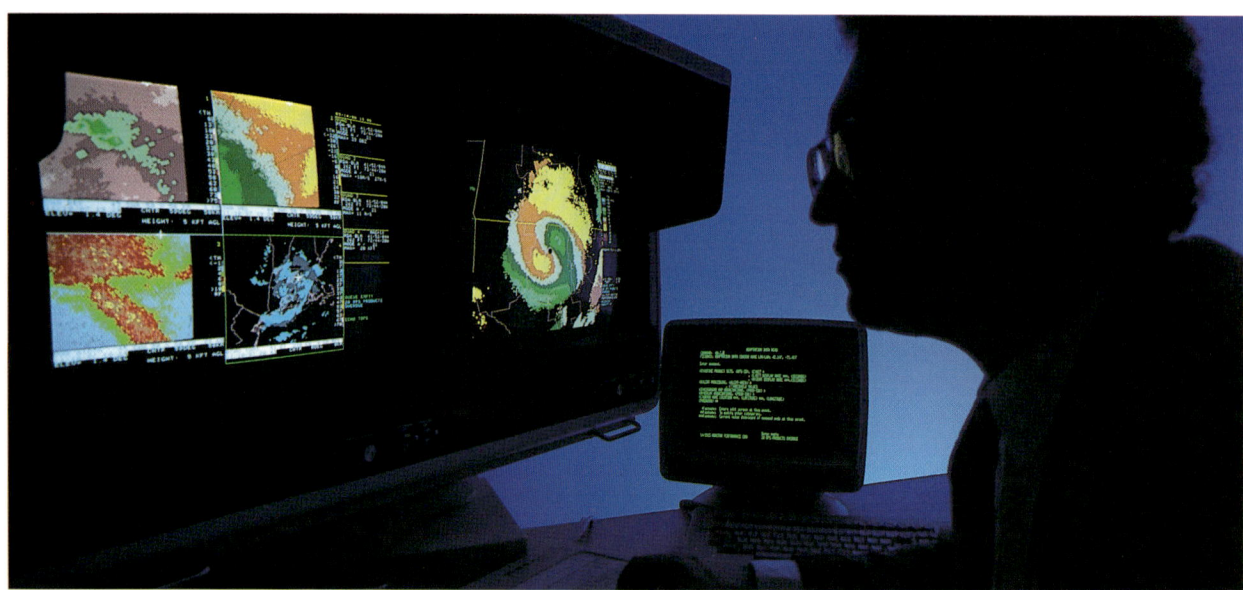

WORLD CLIMATE

In some places, such as deserts or rainforests, the weather is much the same all year round. But in other places, such as northern Europe, the weather can be different every day. The average weather in one place over a long period of time is called the climate.

The climate may include four seasons a year – spring, summer, autumn and winter – or a wet and a dry season. In India, in the winter, winds blow from the dry land to the sea and the dry winter monsoon develops. In summer, winds blow in the opposite direction, from the sea to the land. They pick up moisture from the sea and cause the torrential rain and violent storms of the summer monsoon. If the summer monsoon winds arrive late or do not last very long, the crops may not get enough rain and the people will not have enough to eat. Changes in the weather can be a matter of life or death.

In Australia, the Caribbean and the Far East, very strong winds called cyclones, hurricanes or typhoons can cause terrible damage. These are very large weather systems, which build up in places where there is a lot of warm, moist air. They produce high-speed winds. At the very centre of a cyclone, hurricane or typhoon, there is a circular area of very low pressure with light winds and clear skies. This is called the eye of the storm.

POLLUTION

In the past, the climate of the Earth has always changed. But these changes took place over thousands or millions of years. Nowadays, there is a great danger that people are changing the climate much faster than this because of all the pollution they are putting into the air.

How polluted is the air in your local area? To find out, cut a square from a piece of white cloth and stick a smaller square of cloth onto the middle. Hang your cloth outside for a week or so and then peel off the square in the middle. Is the middle square much cleaner?

You could try putting cloths in different places, such as in the park, by a road or near some factories. What differences can you find?

A lot of the air pollution produced by people is caused by invisible gases. A poisonous mist called smog may develop over large cities such as Los Angeles, London or Tokyo when invisible gases from cars, factories and power stations mix with water in the air. Smog can also be caused by the fumes from car exhausts reacting with sunlight.

One invisible gas that people are putting into the atmosphere could cause an important change in the Earth's weather. This gas is called carbon dioxide. When something is burnt, a lot of carbon dioxide is released into the atmosphere. Power stations, cars and burning rainforests all add carbon dioxide to the atmosphere.

The carbon dioxide acts a bit like the glass in a greenhouse. It traps the heat that rises from the Earth when it is warmed by the sun and stops the heat from escaping into space. This could make the atmosphere warm up and is called the greenhouse effect. If the atmosphere warms up by just a few degrees, this would change the weather, causing the ice caps to melt and land near coasts to be flooded.

MORE THINGS TO DO

Make a wind vane

Have you noticed wind vanes on churches or other tall buildings? They show the direction the wind blows from. To make one yourself, push a length of dowel or a knitting needle into a firm base, such as a cotton reel, a cork wedged in a bottle or a yogurt pot fixed to cardboard with modelling clay. Make labels for the four main compass points (N,S,E,W) and stick these to the base at right angles to each other. Cut an arrow out of thick card and weight the end with a small piece of modelling clay or a paper clip. Glue an old pen top to the arrow and put it on top of the knitting needle or dowel. Make sure the arrow can swing round freely.

Take your wind vane outside and use a compass or the position of the sun in the sky to check that the N,S,E, and W labels are pointing in the right direction. Keep a record of the direction of the wind for a few weeks. From which direction does the wind blow most often? Do strong winds usually blow from one direction?

Wind speed box

Find a small lidded box, such as a shoe box, and cut off both of the short ends. At one end of the box, draw a scale inside the box. Cut a flap out of stiff card and attach it to a piece of dowel or a knitting needle. Push the dowel or knitting needle through the sides of the box so the flap swings to and fro inside the box next to the scale. Put the box outside with the flap end pointing into the wind and keep a record of how far the flap moves along the scale. Draw up a wind speed chart and compare your results with those from an anemometer (see page 21).

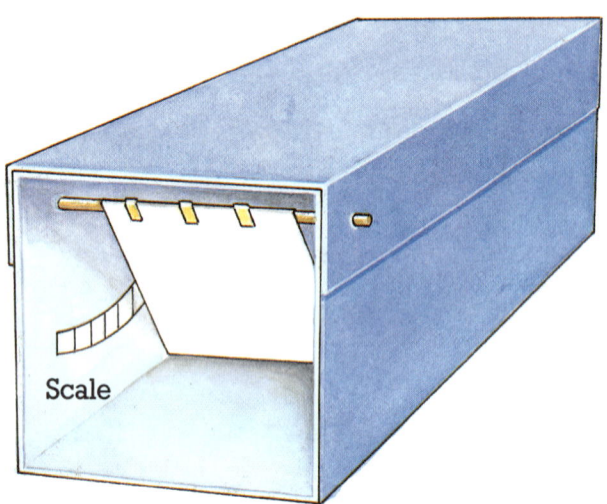

Weather book

Collect weather charts from newspapers over several days or weeks and make a book to show how the weather changes. How many different symbols are used on weather charts? Can you invent your own symbols?

You could also make a scrapbook of cuttings from newspapers or magazines to record disasters caused by weather all over the world. Are some parts of the world more affected by bad weather than others?

Greenhouse effect

To help you understand the basic idea of the greenhouse effect (see page 27), try this investigation. Put two thermometers outside on a sunny day. Cover one thermometer with a big glass jar. Record the temperatures regularly and you should see that it is hotter inside the glass jar, just as it is inside a greenhouse. Repeat this investigation on a cloudy day. Are the results different?

Make a windmill

Cut out four sail shapes or blades from thick card or plastic. Ask an adult to help you make four slits in a cork or a cotton reel and push one sail or blade into each slit. Fix a piece of stiff wire to the cork or cotton reel and fix the wire to an upright piece of wood. Make sure you leave a short length of wire between the cork or cotton reel and the wood. Tie a piece of thread to this wire and fix a weight to the other end of the thread. When you blow on the windmill, can you lift up the weight? Take your windmill outside and see if the wind is more powerful.

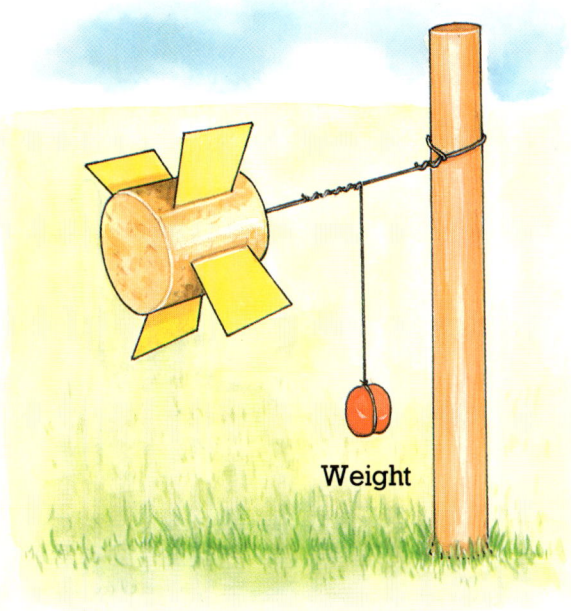
Weight

Powerful air

Place an old ruler on a table so about one third of the ruler sticks out over the edge of the table. Put a flat sheet of newspaper over the top of the ruler. When you strike the ruler sharply with the edge of your hand, what happens?

The air presses down all over the newspaper and this pressure is enough to stop the paper from flying into the air.

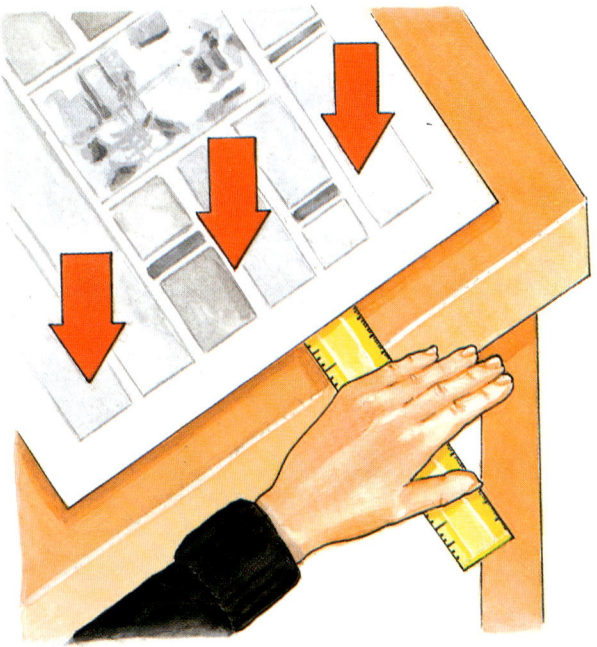

Weather words

See how many words you can think of which describe the weather. Here are a few to get you started: stormy, blustery, squally, blowing a gale, blazing hot, pouring with rain, freezing cold, thunderbolt, typhoon, cyclone. Try to include some words which contain the words wind, rain, sun and snow – for instance, windswept, windbreak, raincoat, snowflake, snowball, sunbeam, sunset. Then write a story or a poem using as many of your weather words as you can. You could also make a weather collage using pictures to illustrate your best words.

DID YOU KNOW?

▲ All the Earth's weather takes place in the lowest part of the atmosphere, which is called the troposphere. This extends upwards from ground level to about 8 kilometres at the poles and about 16 kilometres at the equator. The troposphere contributes about 75 per cent of the weight of the atmosphere.

▲ A hurricane is usually up to 500 kilometres wide and up to 8 kilometres high. The winds in a hurricane reach speeds of more than 150 kilometres per hour. In the Far East, hurricanes are called typhoons. A tornado or "twister" is a column of wind shaped like a funnel. It moves at speeds of up to 80 kilometres per hour over very small areas and can destroy trees and buildings. Winds of at least 330 kilometres per hour have been measured in tornadoes but the winds are too strong to be measured accurately. Tornadoes over 800 metres wide have been recorded in the Midwest of the USA. In Kansas and Oklahoma, there are up to 400 tornadoes each year.

▲ Air pressure is measured in millibars. Air pressure at the surface of the Earth is normally between 960 and 1040 millibars. Readings above 1010 millibars show high pressure and readings below this show low pressure.

▲ In the Northern hemisphere, high pressure areas have winds that blow clockwise around them. Low pressure areas have winds blowing anti-clockwise. In the Southern hemisphere, the winds blow in the opposite direction. This is a result of the forces caused by the spinning Earth, which is called the Coriolis effect.

▲ People have invented lots of different sayings which forecast the weather. Here are some of them: "Red sky at night is a shepherd's delight. Red sky in the morning is a shepherd's warning." "Oak before Ash, we're in for a splash. Ash before Oak, we're in for a soak." "If Candlemas day (2nd February) be fair and bright, winter will have another fight. If Candlemas day brings clouds and rain, winter is gone and won't come again." In the USA, 2nd February is groundhog day. The saying goes, "If the groundhog wakes up and sees his shadow on 2nd February, there will be six more weeks of winter." Can you find out what all these sayings mean? Are they a reliable way of predicting the weather? See how many more weather sayings you can find.

▲ Winds in the Great Storm in S.E. England in October 1987 gusted to 160 kilometres per hour. The strongest recorded wind was 371 kilometres per hour on Mount Washington in north-eastern USA.

▲ Wind-pollinated flowers produce vast amounts of pollen so that at least some of it stands a chance of reaching another flower of the same kind. One birch tree catkin produces up to 5,000,000 pollen grains.

▲ Winds can carry plant seeds many kilometres – an average journey for a dandelion seed is about 10 kilometres.

▲ Air is so light that it takes about 800 bottles of air to weigh as much as one bottle of water. The air in an average classroom weighs as much as a small car.

GLOSSARY

Air pressure
The effect caused by the weight of all the air in the atmosphere pressing down on everything.

Anemometer
An instrument that measures the speed or force of the wind.

Atmosphere
The layer of air that surrounds Earth and is held there by the pull of Earth's gravity. It is made of various gases, mainly nitrogen and oxygen.

Barometer
An instrument that measures air pressure.

Beaufort scale
A scale of numbers representing different wind speeds and a description of their effects on land or sea. It was invented by Admiral Beaufort in the early 19th century.

Climate
The usual weather in a particular place over a long time.

Compressed air
Air which has been squeezed into a small space.

Density
The mass ("weight") of a substance per unit of volume.

Evaporation
The process by which a liquid (such as liquid water) turns into a gas (such as water vapour).

High pressure
A mass of cool, dense air that presses down strongly on the surface of Earth.

Hurricane
A very violent storm that forms over the west Atlantic Ocean around which the winds and clouds swirl in a circle. It is called a typhoon in the Far East and a cyclone in Australia.

Isobar
A line on a weather map that joins places with equal air pressure.

Low pressure
A mass of warm, "light" air which presses down weakly on the surface of Earth.

Millibar
A unit used to measure the pressure of the atmosphere. It is approximately one thousandth of atmospheric pressure.

Pollination
The transfer of pollen from the male part to the female part of a flower or a cone so that seeds can develop. The pollen may be carried by the wind, water or animals, especially insects.

Water vapour
The invisible gas that water turns into when it evaporates.

Wind
A moving mass of air. The movement of the air causes the weather.

Wind erosion
The gradual wearing away of rocks or soil by the force of the wind and particles carried by the wind.

Answer for p. 10:
1 Fuchsia (insects)
2 Grasses (wind)
3 Thistle (insects)
4 Buddleia (insects)

INDEX

air pressure 12, 13, 14, 15, 16, 22, 29, 30, 31
air temperature 16, 17
anemometer 21, 28, 31
Atlantic Ocean 31
atmosphere 4, 13, 14, 22, 27, 30, 31
Australia 25, 31

barchans 8
barometer 15, 31
Beaufort, Admiral 19, 31
Beaufort scale 19, 31
British Isles 22

carbon dioxide 27
Caribbean 25
climate 24, 25, 26, 31
clouds 16, 22, 30
compass 28
compressed air 14, 31
Coriolis effect 30
cyclone 25, 29, 31

density 16, 31
deserts 8, 25

Earth 4, 13, 26, 27, 30, 31
energy 7
England 30
equator 30
erosion 8, 31
evaporation 5, 31

Far East 25, 30, 31
forecasting 22, 30
friction 9

gale 19, 29
gases 27, 31
gravity 13, 31
Great Storm 30
greenhouse effect 27, 29

high pressure 14, 16, 17, 30, 31
humidity 22
hurricanes 19, 25, 30, 31

India 25
isobars 14, 31

Kansas 30

London 27
Los Angeles 27
low pressure 14, 16, 17, 25, 30, 31

meteorologists 22
millibar 31
monsoon 25

nitrogen 31

Oklahoma 30
oxygen 31

plants 10, 11, 30
poles 30
pollination 10, 30, 31
pollution 7, 26, 27
power stations 7, 27

rain 25, 29
rainfall 22
rainforests 25, 27

sails 6, 7
satellites 22
seeds 10, 11, 30, 31
smog 27
snow 29
storms 19, 22, 25, 29, 31
sun 16, 17, 27, 28, 29

temperature 22
thermometers 29
Tokyo 27
tornado 30
troposphere 30
twister 30
typhoon 25, 29, 30, 31

USA 30

Washington 30
water 4, 8, 13, 27, 31
water vapour 5, 31
weather balloons 22
weather stations 22
windmills 7, 29
wind direction 20, 22, 28
wind power 6
wind socks 20
wind speed 19, 20, 21, 22, 28, 31
wind vane 28

Additional photographs:
BBC Photograph Library 14; The Environmental Picture Library 27 (b); European Space Agency/Science Photo Library 23; Frank Lane Picture Agency 25; Robert Harding 24; Eric and David Hosking 19 (t); Stephen Krasemann/NHPA 19 (b); Helene Rogers/Trip 20 (t); ZEFA 6 (t), 7 (b), 8, 9, 11, 22, 27.
Picture Researcher: Ambreen Husain

32